gospel

of

regicide

eunsong kim

gospel

of

regicide

eunsong kim

Book Cover Design: Jimena Sarno
Book Interior Design: Sarah Gzemski
Cover Image by Eunsong Kim, the photograph is from a collaborative project
with artist Katy Collier

The Gospel of Judas, published by the National Geographic Society, translated
by Rodolphe Kasser, Marvin Meyer, and Gregor Wurst, in collaboration with
François Gaudard appears on page 17, 18, 19, 23 and 31. Page 17 also contains
language from the Wikipedia page on The Gospel of Judas.

The lines in quotations and some in italics are from the following texts:

The Gospel of Judas, *Some Questions of Moral Philosophy* by Hannah Arendt,
Whiteness as Property by Cheryl Harris, the King James Bible, "Theses on the
Philosophy of History" by Walter Benjamin, and a press statement from Pope
Ratzinger

Published by Noemi Press, Inc. A Nonprofit Literary Organization.
www.noemipress.org.

wholly for Helen Oam

Contents inside:

Regicide

The Gospel

regicide

HE

he was either a demon
or holy unrecognized

either an "eccentric fringe"
or truth you were denied

either the marked unbeliever
or reason for your salvation

either conspiracy
or you have loved him through lies

how simple and clean this love of money

how clean and direct the story of money

i have long black hair and freckles and what looks like smooth skin and eyes with so much black in them and it's all so nondescript

you believe i could be her or her or that other her so when you come up and say hey Nancy, hey Candice, hey Sarah I say hey and walk away.

i look like all of them so i know when the police smile at me they are smiling at them.

my shirts are crispy. they are crispy and i have lots of them and i smile on sight i smile a lot so you don't believe i am really planning to kill you. i hate everything about your presence. i do not say this i just smile and nod.

please remember this whenever someone who looks like me smiles and nods.

found to tear, found because burials found before space
before flight and mends before it all you have been part of this
body

the best and only reason for things to end

is that there is no love

But for you, savior

Here is all of my love

He visited me behind an envelope. I tore his name away to
wear it as a nametag alongside the ribcages below my eyes, the
ones that sprout when touched to say that there is too much
of me in this world.

How the lines from the right have changed from the left. If
the scars below the bows have faded, changed in numbering,
disappeared.

Father in heaven the broken cannot be traded cannot be
traded Father on earth on heaven the words that follow the
mouthings father

    Forever and ever into my dreams

Elsewhere in the manuscript

He favors Judas above

by saying:

Step away from the others &

I shall tell you the mysteries of the kingdom:

You have been told everything.

The star that leads your way is the star—

Judas:

I know who you are and where you have come from.

I am not worthy to utter

the name of the one who has sent you.

But when he said this,

He left him.

deliver us from whiteness
from its benevolent privatization
deliver us from the anecdotal rapture
was yesterday not also the apocalypse—
deliver us from their imagination
from the constant circulation of their language:
you are all the same.
deliver us from their glories
from what they describe as kingdom and
beauty and art. and comedy. tragedy. style. warmth. fullness
openness candor dessert image imagery movement ideas
violence particularly violence protection softness stealth
silence

Let not one trace survive.

a world without them: Haven

Stories that do not remember them

Home.

traitors believe in another kind of death, flesh, kingdom
traitors are told such tales and then
traitors tell themselves these stories
they say
he wanted me to
they say
i needed the money fuck off
they say
he wasn't what we needed
they say
sacrifice only pleases the lower gods and some of the angels
you are missing the point
they say
you are missing the point
they have every story every idea every poem
memorized in defense
traitors come prepared
traitors are more prepared than you are
you are nothing in contrast to the
poetry flooding inside the traitor's flesh

sacrifice is for the lower level gods, those not ready and those

that just don't get it.

They approached

Judas and said

What are you doing here?
You are his disciple.

Judas answered
                        as they wished.

And received
some money

and handed him over to them.

I did everything to come home.

A plot to love you save you lose myself

A plot to be debated a plot without faith an excavated plot

a plot all ours

a plot just ours

Arendt States:

Judas Iscariot, the greatest example of mortal sin, went and hanged himself.

Religiously (not morally) speaking, it seems that
they must all be forgiven because
they did
not know
what they were
doing.

Pound scribbles, *And no indulgence at Judas's tree*

kiss me kiss me kiss me

Traitor isn't the one with a nice house moderate debt brunch
buddies

Traitor as that which becomes erased, remembered only
through their gossip their scorn

Who can plead no forgiveness

Who rests best as conspiracy

Nostalgia

Uncatalogued

Monster

How long does it take to become a monster

How many kills how many lies how many

How long does it take and

Why is this the only name you can find for me

This is only my first kiss

betrayal makes having been born not worth it
the bible says
betrayal makes life
not worth it

woe unto that man by whom
the Son of man is betrayed!

It would have been good for that man
if he had not been born.

how absolutely, absolutely
adorable

Since you kissed him in sixth grade and learned to drink three bottles at a time. And no one had to say a word but the debt was there and the houses got smaller the phone calls longer. And months at a time people disappeared as you put on your uniform and left for school in the mornings and then to untaxed jobs that hired your face. And the system is different. The language doesn't fit we never spoke so these are words through someone else's mouth. Collected leftovers. And there was no money and someone whispered factory and you dropped everything and came home. Sat in a room for a year with books you couldn't read to enter a school no one could afford. It didn't matter anyway. They would take you to an island anyway. The theory was that you would be better adjusted in this small place with no body in it and find a baby. Two baby faces. Staring across imagination. As we pass each other with riddles (no more lofty) dreams of crossing the blue sea for a new language of course I read the bible. In addition to weekend language school, my mother would watch me hand copy pages of the korean bible. I wrote slowly. I used the bathroom often tried to make conversation would get into trouble and then the afternoon would be about my insolence: bible copying would be set-aside for the following weekend. I may have written most of the old testament. Hello Numbers.

yes I read the bible. In english. In english for clarity. And won a few rounds of local bible competitions. For proof I did have some trophys. I had trophys but as I was moving I threw them out. I threw them out with the yearbooks, dance team tights, negatives I purged my life like this was a possibility.

I am always purging my life set on this possibility.

He said to them,

How do you know me?

no generation of the people
among you will know me.

just cuz we shared some miracles and you talked about your
sins does not mean you know me.

THE DISCIPLES BECOME ANGRY

When his disciples heard this, they started getting
angry and began blaspheming against him in their
hearts.

Wait are you playing hard to get? Did all those years of sacri-
fice and miracle witnessing mean nothing to you?

He was the youngest son they were too poor
No
He was most ambitious his family couldn't let him stay
No
He escaped on a hidden train car came with nothing
No
He spoke too many languages yes
He worked at their embassy yes
At 18 he was not an anti-colonialist yes
At 18 he ran south
He ran and said nothing and died before we could ask him
questions yes
He was a translator yes
So the other side

Yes?

the possibilities of non-growth based economies—the possibility in gathering negatives in order to construct neutrals (rather than its surplus).

an occupation that requires portions of my body to be revealed and for my body to be engaged in traditional service activities—in exchange for high valued gratuities.

this durational performance will not engage in sex work—as this work does not wish to make abstract an occupation that has already become abstracted and filled with the metaphors of others.

a performance that will fuck the aura and meaning of sacrifice and punishment and will actively speak on behalf of my body—if ever violence becomes present.

while I accrue an acceptable and needed amount of currency, the organization that installs this performance will contact individuals (they will be kept anonymous from myself and the performance) who have become obsessed and disillusioned by personal debt.

there will be a criterion stating the kinds of debt that will and will not be acceptable for participation.

desiring participants cannot bring forth business accrued debt, gambling debt, the debts of others.

the currency acquired by this occupational performance will be managed by the organization and immediately paid to the participant's respective debt accounts—until the accounts no longer require payment. When full debt payments are reached, all parties involved will sign contracts to abstain from future contact. And the durational performance will continue for another participant.

At this moment, there is no time limit for this performance.

The performance will proceed until my desires for debt have been fulfilled, nullified.

lingerie site newsletter announcements
rent a camera for twenty five percent off
record the reoccurring rapture
with an IPL facial you'll be prettiest for the
end of times photo shoot
surely sparkling at the protest
press & breeze through
one delivered us an evil afternoon:

in crouching tiger she jumps
in bungeejumping they jump
where else

off the frame
can we follow

Looking for the frames to follow

I'm working on a story that I might include in this volume
about a series of girls who are out for revenge (great gals).
There is a girl who finds out her partner is collecting debt
from an ex, a girl who is an actress, a girl who is married and
on a mission to take the company down—my girls.

Forever dreaming of who they might hunt next

So here I am in the meta prelude. Dreaming of how else to
dream them

These are not confessions this is not a confession

They are a collection of revisions upon revisions that roam my memories which means they

are utter lies and my only foundation

the gods know that the only way to move the revolution
forward is to

have a man kiss you

and take you to your enemies

If it is for love *I'll* stay
an animal.
an easy metaphor

I know the ghost is you. But help me look anyway.

remove the umbrella stems. spread the holding dots.

i wrote something here but deleted it because i realized that it's just going to bring me more direct, personalized harassment.

but this deletion will not be permanent. this deletion is temporary.

so just that we're clear in this deletion, if we don't say your name immediately, we don't address you immediately

i will say your name directly at some point before i die

what reasonings do they give

what do they say about her childhood

she loves only money doesn't she

ungrateful cunt makes being born not worth it

she makes living his life

not worth it

that's how wonderful she is

he says

i'm worried that you'll turn on me

are you turning on me

Personne stands at the door.
One open door, two feet of space, one person standing.
Seethingly I say, pointing at the shoes.
For runaways. I see.

Buy me some shoes. My wish is to be half like you.

What does she look like
The ghost you write about.

Ghosts have long black hair
Blue skin
And red lips.
Like you

A separate collection of notebooks
A catalogue of accounts
What we spend
What we buy
Obsessed to record
Evidence of together—

No, wait,
Take me for free
I've been stained and
Have reduced my fees.

No longer desiring to spy
vulnerabilities
preparing for the day
Makeup blouses tights heels
roaming
seeking
small white envelopes
where money once contained.

Metaphors Fully Consumed:

Shadows
Models
Mannequins
All kinds of waters
Dark skies
Bright skies
(Adjective) hearts
Extinct & animal
Young girls
Young boys
Jump cuts
Waiting periods
Stagnation
Lost things
Black frames
Machine guns
Fireworks
Dessert
Sand
Clocks
Assassins
(to be continued...)

For this life.

Promise to find me first in our next—

In English for Clarity

I.

I asked for a confession father   speak of the current image that haunts   of the evolved memories I write on though this is not of today remember each one of these booths are covered in traded colors   in pigments of someone else's memories   Father   in mine they range   in mine the confessions are pressed from bees   their colors are drops of hot iron clashes yellow ironed by steam and night   polished by water   I   can hear their wings flutter as they become the bodies for a wholly covered space   you hear the mutters of things cloistered and black   a wanting for flesh   of mother

II.

The remnants I no longer believe   the words that float inside without the pretension of release Father your loneliness this empty church is my answer my mother *All that is destroyed is my love*   don't ask don't repeat *tell me* I treasure the copies with original envy with majesty reserved for a tourist this way when I say help you cannot pretend to misunderstand you cannot turn to the other two in a different language and respond simply with
      How still you feel How closely this resembles love. Father even violence can be redeemed this way. When enclosed in this much solitude. In this temperature and Mother it has much to do with age and never being mine. But what I have to say is fluent
      the consistency of my concerns are fluent

The Golden

Yes, for someone poor you grew up nicely. Clever and unlike your kind. But it is true that you were raised in another country. I have already repeated to my daughter that it is a country full of feathers but no birds. It is what happens outside of this place.

There are 10,000 boys for sale who look just like you. Went to the same schools. Speak the same singular language. Share the same expressions, facially. I am reasoning rationally, and your level of writing and reading will transform your definition of sacrifice.

You may get what you plotted to take. You are counting my white hairs I see. I count on many things.

Such as—Loneliness is a mnemonic device.

The inheritance of palindromes

Digital Threnody

a poem cannot solve tonight
however much i worship her

a poem does not solve but i read another anyway
the title states it's about the apocalypse
from yesterday.

each couplet his shoulders
an acquaintance with beauty towards his refrain
inner rhymes peering into steady oceans
his fears his wants his thoughts
not one cloaked metaphor (kindness)
his hair his lovers his jeans him   him   him   him
the disaster rectified in the witnessing of his collarbones
his square
unbroken
jaw
finished.

i want to kill him. i close my eyes
to invent the scenarios
i plead
poem kill him.

all of my dreams involve a murder
an eating of tongues

and yet the day's news of these exact events—

the anathema is a poem i call my own
that could have been written by him
amen

Shaman

The shells of a very white peach and not a picture   could have been adolescencing all things subtle. It makes remembering softer to see them as ghosts. Othello: It is cruel to compare her to a failed celebrity. Cruel to seek her through in that kind of an afterlife. When her and the other vessels of transported labor have chosen the life as a cook to suffice. For the right temperament in exchange, it is the value price of stains.   If her letter can be paraphrased it is this: Acting not like a stranger is becoming harder. Sometimes she needs to pause and look at a map, ask for repetition, but she doesn't. It is her colony after all. This loss is better than that of a fires

The Lovers

To all the non-aggression pacts declined,
The media coverage you deserved:

This is in frame accordance. White sheets wrapping to kiss. Each girl in a rose colored top.
Each gentleman in a suit

their shadows falling at the mouth against backdrops used to document weddings, black
market kinds. The green too green since there is no honeymoon.

Truth has made a comeback. Has convinced us to repeat her name.

But you've never seen this picture. We brushed by it once at the door. You looked straight
the other way. I said left. And you turned around to inanimate objects

that float by us through the screens scripting our future dialogue, endings.

Soft Soaps: *All About Bali*

I.

gramsci reference check. explanation of hegemony check. the importance of a love triangle check. queer transitional objects. critique of transnational capital. the deconstruction of abstraction & value. exposing the consolidation of corporate power check. the affective powers of the proletariat check.

check check check.

2.

please be sure to insert a marketable piece of jewelry
that the long lost lovers lost
or members of the triangles give to one another
so that we might negotiate with the various vendors
on the appropriate brand/object placement
—thank you in advance

3.

Does she understand:

social climbing doesn't work!
SOCIAL CLIMBING WORKS

4.

Lied to keep you
Ill
Fallen
Capitalist
Broken to keep you

5.

he tells her:

I see myself in you
I see how our bodies work
for the same machine

                    everything except marry you—

6.

ask for a yacht
the summer house
an island! ten universities!
dump the shopping and
ask for the military
what are you doing?

7.

I did it for debt
Debt did it for me.
He paid and
We paid and
There you are.
On the screen so
Don't forget
Now that it's gone.

8.

the poor and the vermin
plot the revolution
because it's the sexy thing to do:

a see saw for character
a water slide in lieu of character

9.

How many voices do you have inside
brain trauma, forgetting, I don't remember how to remember
plastic surgery, orphanages, war—

10.

first you must endure my humiliation
            a body carved through errors
            no glorification of errors
then the contract
then, and after then
the longing

11.

only the errors are mine

12.

One—clean—precise—uncomplicated

Trade

For a

A generation of girls who repeat:

Gumihos

She never appeared that way in front of me she was always young and classifiably breedable. Black hair, that kind of skin, and and

In picture books they drew her in twos. Her and the soul she wanted kept in jars, lockets, hearts yes. Yes. In picture books my mother read, Read: stay away from her. Too beautiful to be trusted but too beautiful to forget. She takes your soul and keeps them in jars and things. Stories to teach you to stay close to your mother. Stories to teach you to marry, even earlier than you desired.

Animals that work all their goddamn lives to be human. Mostly failing because human stories want them to. Animals baring, laboring, harboring this disguise for a life defined by transitional disguises. Animals desiring to be human

To spare you the details, the ingredients to become a human are as follows:

1. Nine souls of unmarried men—We do not discriminate nor is there a preference. We're open to all shapes and sizes. Honestly.

2. One large and sturdy enough container to hold them all—

Once the ingredients are secured She is allowed to trade for a permanent position. A permanent body to sleep in.

Have I skipped too many details. Do you need more. I'm trying to paraphrase the stories about the wolves that wanted to become women. And all the humans in between that have broken the rules.

Of course we met when she had all 8. And the 8, I'm assuming, were relatively easy to find. She joked once that number 6 was so desperate to see more of her skin that he gave his up voluntarily. She traded her mirage for the possession of their unused souls. But after seeing number 6 disappear so quickly and collapse pathetically on the hotel floor she wondered if she was preying a bit. Preying on the weak, the ignorant the confused. Preying on those that watched too much television and had a difficult time speaking. To anyone. Preying on those that never liked girls at all so never made the effort and then She comes along—simplifying the steps. Truly, sincerely, preying.

When she told me all of this she was out of breath and angry—so most of this is what I think she was trying to say in between breaths. You could never understand, she said, wanting what I want. You already have it, she repeated. So how could you want it?

I told her that I'm sure number 6 died happily, with the image of her two bosoms in mind and the thought of sex with Her. How could he have died sadly? I would be just as willing! It is an exit. The exit is for us. You didn't take anything from anyone. They, we gave them to you. But everything I said just reminded her of number 6's thump and of childhood sacrifices and how much she hated anything to do with a sacrifice. Well that's just nuts, I told her. What did you think a trade was?

All of the difficulties involved in killing me number 9 and the recent epiphany about sacrifices drove her into a shopping frenzy. Four days into her transformation deadline she found herself at various shopping centers, an hour into their final hour, craving "mature pineapple farm" nail polish, socks with various dessert images, and pastel stationeries. All the items listed and more and then four multicolored mini-binoculars later, she realized that none of these products were going to make sense in her wolf pack community, hunting and hiding and all—and whether or not her decision to shop was her own. Anonymous pastel thank-you letters to family members, notifications for helping a "person" solidify desired existence. It would be one way to confess. *Thank you for helping me, I'm sad number 4 never finished college, but in return, I will get my masters!* It could say. It could say.

The shopping
The missing
The taking
The lying in bed
The waiting the waiting
The blue smoke
She's sick already

But she couldn't. No matter how hard I tried, she couldn't.

The fable of the wolf wanting to be a human
Has the possibilities of an anticapitalist tale
Return to the forest
Don't take what is not yours
Even when they say yes
It also has the possibilities of upper-class Buddhist Teachings
Ignore the violence &
Concentrate on frogs
Stay as you are &
Grow inside

But in the end
Even though I can.
And you've agreed
It is not worth it
To take it from you

Turn me into a water ghost instead
A traveling soul in water
Instead

Regicide

I.

By the time you were
The proletariat
Version of yourself
The version you were always meant to be
How could we love you the same

Tell me how you were able to survive this way
Picking for your food
Resting on hours to determine your days

Tell us
How we are to adore you—Now

II.

My desire for regicide
My desire for the throne to be empty
Unseated always in my presence

Missionary Tells

I.

More interested in displaying remains of her heart

Than moving forward success

She would sit ministers down and demand full confessionals

It's important that we empty ourselves

Before proceeding. She would lie in front of them

Pleading to their shoes asking for his job back

They left she packed. They left

She packed.

Her field research is on exorcism he told me *That's what she needs to concentrate on*

A lifelong project to protect the possessed from the weak

They call for her. She is the only one burnt, burning twice as theirs.

She can hide them and grow them and cure them and even if there is no autobiography

Let's hope that the once possessed cultivate a memory.

They kicked us out

We became too critical of the deadlines

The apocalypses that refused to pass

We gave away our stockpiled water, rice, beans to the neighbors across the street

We were supposed to bring them back.

We didn't do anything right.

The man downstairs

He helps us from time to time with the rent

He doesn't have any children or something like that

So he offered to help us

So if we leave now where will we go

We know that he'll take care of us

You can leave us here and it wouldn't matter.

You're not the only ones with money.

On her honeymoon her husband casually asked her to lose weight

Right before dinner he sat her down and asked her to look outside

Jeju where servant girls accompanied

The thickest of blood intellectuals

The island of female pearl divers who kept the exiled alive

The men who continued to write books about justice

He asked her to look at the women on the streets

And count the number of girls thinner than her

If there is less than five than you can stay the way you are

He has a nice smile and holds onto his words

All his life he has been called kind. All his life women have called him kind.

II.

You're right.
god wanted to pay for that nose
all those bitches are gonna shout but he wanted to raze both chins, push them in
to stretch your eyes widest
some bitches get that shit done and they can never shut their eyes again
but god knew
that the better you would be waiting, waiting, planting, saving
he wanted you to be old enough to understand that
all choice is really his
so when those other clanks throw shoes at you
and ask for their offering back
you tell them you didn't grow vegetable gardens in Kazakhstan for fifteen years to
pluck the wrong nose.
You tell them that they can plant seeds too.
No one told them to be middle class waiting at a clinic for some miracle
There are scalpels and there is fidelity: then both.
god knows how to take care of girls who code both—

Messiah

Slits
opened by curiosity
The impossibility of paralleling our legs
Why we search for things beneath
Why we think you might return
The scientist's mistake
Professional eyeliner
Portals to you
Bits of light to remind us
Red that refuses
The manner in which you remain
Unredacted
In which you understand who is looking
Who is watched
It is this manner
Quoted from memory
From darker to more present
And more present to failing
These are the etiquettes
That you bestial
Every collected caesura in the world

Purge Song

I have explained to self that
NC-17 exists
in place of poems
that skin suffices
as border pillaging
more would be a cascade
more leads to conquer
more to surrender

the parts kept
are the scraps that did not make it as marrow

the written parts kept
—unrequited capitulation.

A Purge Song:

my matriarchs did not suffer quietly
for me to die symbolically this kind

but in every timeline it's you

Working Towards 31 Letters and 13 Dreams

you are in front of their hands, the sculpture
you want to buy it and look in your coin purse
it is flooded with notes and reminders and letters you swore to never read again
you think it will never end and skip home
you are trying to manage yourself in this breakup but you are behind on paperwork
you are paid hourly, here, still
you do not hear from them but is that so different, has so much changed, here?
you cup your forehead and tug your ears.
three dark moons later you read about the hands in a villa loved by racist and their kind
you want to wake up you want to see them you want to touch them
but you are in front of a map at a compass store muttering to yourself about a heist
you walk into the bathroom and cry into the window
if you wake up you know what is possible
when you wake up will you know what is possible.

You take a Greek mythology course and learn about women who wait
men roamed—your beautiful professor tells you
women wait.
you know there's a gender critique but you don't care and split
your head open in hopes of someone born not of a man
you think of every fight you've had and paint your nails a mermaid color
and begin packing
you remember the superstition that instructs
against buying lovers: shoes
they'll run away they say
you want to ask them to take you but you believe they already know
so you say nothing
you have a boat four umbrellas and a salt water aquarium filled with brooches
you pack it all

you never wanted to say goodbye but here you are
in love with how many runaways

you find photographs of them together. worse, they are solitary portraits of him.
eyes for them you are to assume
your high school bully and your person.
all those closed doors subrosa communiqué: town gossip explodes.
you don't know where you are but you have to admit it's a little hot.
pummeled yet practical you are.
you cannot find a way to wake until the next day's discovery.
you spend a week and a half working on a letter to send them.
the first draft was set a year ago the second draft happened on your phone. the draft from
last week was shrill. on the 6th day it is cordial. self-effacing.
limited with a touch of emotion.
so they do not think of you as a clay android.
you dream and dream you send the letter and they agree. you dream and dream that you
send this cordial, self-effacing, limited yet touched letter and
you ask them does anything remind me of you—would you tell me?
you talk to yourself. you have another chat. you say: it is just one dream.
drop it:
you can try.
when you wake up and the photographs disappear your glasses found all drafts sent one
dream dropped picture and bed intact
you place the note on my forehead
dear Chiron:
could you speak to me today—

you are asked to read at a poetry reading and you say yes. they send the list of readers. you respond. you ask—with the civility you can muster—are you to understand that you are the only non white reader? you state you are not asking for a "diversity" treatment. they respond: this is a white city (no) there are very few poets of color here (no). they respond: we thought of one other person of color, they will read with you.

you respond. you state that you will be unable to attend the event. you lie, it's true. there are no personal emergencies other than the reoccurring apocalypse of white supremacy but you lie and say: there is a personal emergency because you do not have the energy to write a longer email. you do not have the energy to explain. why should you explain. they respond: you have always been disrespectful. they respond: you are a bully. they respond: this is detrimental. they respond: most poets are flattered by reading requests. they respond: we tried to be diverse. they respond: this is unpaid work—this herding of you—is unpaid work.

you do not respond because it has already swallowed your day and it cannot be continued. you do not respond but there are things to say such as: yes, I am disrespectful. great. a bully. a perfect word: detrimental. so. fucking. ungrateful are you. am I. for whom is this paid work and is obedience receipt of payment? for whom is this work paid? you do not respond.

you dream you write a different letter
you begin by telling them about the joke Anne made when you told her
and she responded by revising: it is not "For My Lover, Returning to His Wife"
it's "Lover, No Wife—Returning: Simply Returning"
you cannot defend yourself
you are inside a fragment inside the shard of a live romantic comedy
playing the part of a mistress
you know
the kind described as disposable
that we snicker at in amusement
the kind that tells you about the *potential* of the romance

the waiting woman
in need of clairvoyance
written without conclusion
eat us alive you scream
tear us apart

you meet anne again at the park and she comments on your droppy lids
you think this is racist but you say nothing because even in your dreams you think: what
would be the point
you say nothing but you return no *compliment*
when you meet an older journalist for lunch five years later, which is a million years in
cauchemar time
you tell him about this incident you say
how could she have been a great poet
she was unabashedly racist
and he chuckles and as his gesture of solidarity
tells you how she was beautiful, when she was younger
you know, hahahaha, before she expired
white people are always trying to teach you, encouraging you to commodify your misery
the best of them say: we commodify your misery, why not learn how to do it for yourself!
the best of them believe they are helping you set up a small business, a non-profit yes yes!
two windows, some slot for money, narration of all the moments you cannot remember you
cannot profess without crying: repeat
you are still in front of the compact mirror
you are climbing all the wrong stairs
you are jumping off another fractured timeline
you are thinking about the second lunch
you are thinking of your slotted face
you think about fixing her how can you fix her better
you are thinking about growing it, killing it

all the other girls are doing it: you can try
enough you think and take an oath with the virgin huntress
you are slaughtered by her devotees in less than two hours
that's how soon they find you
that's how fast you burst

kindness are you moist.

to vaporate this way

you hear three poems where
drones are personified
they giggle
they accidentally drop things
they metaphor
you witness an Asian American poet reading such a poem
and you raise your hands
you ask
what are the ethical stakes
of abstracting a military weapon
first manuals in english
invented, utilized and deployed
with non-english targets in mind
the drone flies, you scream
towards cities and names many of us can barely pronounce
you drop them on your page as a risk factor
the bikini in the airline commercial
anathemas
you are an anathema

she says nothing but she has been smiling.
she grips the mic near her crossbody accessory
touches the ends of her hair, smiling, and thanks you for your comment
including that she only wanted a new device for her panda to sit on, and thought of it hu-
morously
she intended no harm, she states nodding
you predict they will laugh but there is no unison. there is no unison
but there is no collapse

you are shaking you are shaking and hoping you are alone
and hoping that the auditorium has grown since
that record was pressed and photographs were taken
that when your name is entered and shaken all anyone will remember is

asian

    —alienate

    & mystify

    feels like

    but has never been yours

    speech that could be a poem

    if written by *you*:

    conduit for reserved for

    for whom does your body make easy

—american.

Pending Protest Guides

1.

whiteness as property
whiteness as expansion
whiteness and freedom which
freedom as expansion
whiteness the police state
whiteness as property
Cheryl Harris: the absence of whiteness "meant being the object of property"
which
the vastness of history this absence
everlasting fits into this exclusion called absence
the object of property

2.

1991 sentencing for Latasha Harlins's murderer:
5 years probation
400 hours community service
500 dollar fine

2016 sentencing for Akai Gurley's murderer:
5 years probation
800 hours community service
(-----)

x number of probation years
some community service
a petty fine, no time anywhere, inside

state payment for
for, for, for—

3.

Ellen Wu defines model minority as the construction of: *definitively not black*

Definitively not Black working towards the good life

4.

identification without solidarity
solidarity as theft is the history of how much organizing
coalition to address all concerns equally for equal mounts of time infomercial sales
coalition lead by middle positions tech start up model

identification: peripatetic
solidarity: sacred
coalition: holy, failing, holy failing

5.

miscarriage world:

the umbrella is traumatic you see

6.

the narrative of criminality: accepted
the everlasting visibility of evidence: denied as proof

7.

one tragedy
two victims?

8.

one tragedy
one victim

9.

inabilities to count
propensity against true names

Translating Lineage

the first time i heard the phrase "호적에서 판다"
was a pre IMF soap opera.
i've heard it since, in family arguments
during fights in restaurants
"I will remove you from the lineage"
is how it might translate
or perhaps
from the lineage you will be expunged

often the accused will respond, *sure*
go ahead
displaying their ambivalence to the lineage, their ability to remain
calm during hurricanes, ultimatums
recognition for the accuser to remove the accused. a fancy
a drawing:
a possibility

to refashion your lineage in *a moment of danger.*

war, second families
north selectors who never returned
constructed property
orphans sent away
immigrants without papers
stolen persons

outside the lineage and
made outside of the lineage

poetry as archive for those without lineage
poetry as loom for those without lineage

treacherous present for the only future imaginable—

*

the act of denying the father
is to peer into one's records and
situate first the enslaved

                          and then all others

the

gospel

Clepsydras

I. Humid, in thoughts with other shoes

I. Letters some mother writes, identical in content so understandably easier to carve to continue

I. A bee keeper's hat, black silk that longs for transparency, comfortable nude platforms.

I. How my tongue becomes affected by this plate.

I. Cheekbones that grip like warm butter closer to

I. The time please, I need the time.

I. The birth of a birth inside a palindrome

II. Second names names thereafter

II. As hard as unread Braille

III. Medea is impossible unless we are too much in the sun

III. Comedians say to Magicians "Better than a lifetime in a hat"

IV. My feyed Sphinx.

IV. (1) Rising pink ribbons (2) proper letters of reference

V. It is to describe you, dearest.

I. A permanent pen, as permanent as possible before effacement.

I. The compromise is, your name, my wrist.

I. That kind of oblivion, variegated.

I. To count the time from the womb, officially, in government documents.

I. Made coral for Irredention.

I. A resistance to tattoos and fixtures, primary colors.

I. My wiled Sphinx. It's the only way we know how.

A Love For Violence

intoxication of futuris
izm
mysterious feelings
a body of velvet
asexual manners
morals

in a tin box
reflecting colors
similar to a dry
cleaned rainbow

a thrown away image
pull apart years hiding nothing but ellipses

farewell my heart
we are barely enough
remains.

The Gospel

i've been wanting to write an epic on treachery. the love it requires.
its militancy
it's gendered formations (the woman, the vengeful woman,
the woman in love, the woman who hates)
how when she appears there are no questions
we just say: oh yes. ah her. yeah we know her. take her away.

i want to write an ode to her. and how becoming
her is the only goal in a resurrected life—

Judas. That muthafucker who sold out for silver coins. Probably didn't even negotiate. The cop-ilk were like: this bag of 30 and Judas said whatever. I guess during the apocalypse I will pay rent and splurge on last season's croc bow sandals, matching coin purse. They were like: here is your silver and he said: yeah, whatever.

Never fully believed anyway. I'm a patriot so.

This is what they state in dictionaries, in bible studies, all kinds of pop songs. They say: don't be Judas. Be Noah be Abraham be Jacob be Paul be any other man, but don't be her.

Judas the betrayer. The unbeliever. Judas the doubter. Judas who only wanted some silver.

Judas the reason our beloved was crucified—

Imagine my surprise when I'm sitting in an artist lecture by an Asian American artist who at some point says that aesthetics and politics are separate. I write in my notes: *Kant lover <3 <3 <3, whatever loser, you suck die*

He then goes on to utter phrases that sound like they come out of an assimilationist handbook. things like: i don't really think about race and race doesn't really affect me and other such phrase to silence to wound

And then, as if splitting from himself—he ends on a note on betrayal. He talks about the Gospel of Judas: some say Judas betrayed god because he was asked to. Judas was selected, as his most devoted disciple, as the only disciple that could hold the secret and act the part of banishment, as the only disciple that needed no text, no fame, no ever after in our imaginations, as the only disciple to say, yes: crucify me upside down

Trigger the insurrection. complete the story.

And she, tasked with the image and act of betrayal, loved enough to say yes

So here we are. god worshipped as the returning son because of Judas and her love betrayal.

Mark 5:33

I.
We find scarves on the streets
for our wives.
white strips hanging from a
tree whose toys, whose feet

whose surrender courts near

not our gifts,
we agree.

II.
She—
stood behind.
waiting

Could not request
as she was formed.

so
kneeling
she sought
To be perfected
through thoughts.

III.
Allow
before catastrophe
before resolutions

Allow
miracles as prevention
propaganda as gold mines
all foundational, rudimentary tactics of
a new small small business

IV.
The Ad campaigned could say:

He turns
He turns to her
He felt
She did not need more than she had already
touched
and could live now in
true divinity—

Judgment Tales

—Fraudulence as perfume, as potion, as a passion/life choice

— Same tone racists: you cannot catch: sex

— The Samsung executive and his daughter's suicide, his absence at her
   funeral

— Make-up and, And

— The perfect significant: is chipped a hundred percent, always by choice.
   Peel by peel the metals show, pre-ordered fantasies jump start the processes
   inside

—Origins of petty power

—Megalomaniacs and their fourteen year olds

—Alterations found in such reproduced structures

—I've only known one version all my life

—and look

—another

it's sickening, isn't it? it's sickening and full

so full so full so

full so

Copy Paper

I envisioned you to be
a dulled silver,
rounded fingertips
strongest glass
overlaid for nails
surprisingly happy in
this predicament

As you touch me
I feel
my skin, or the lightness
that comes with my own.

You touch my shoulder to
tell me that your arms
are much too long
that as you close around
You can feel them more
than you can feel my spines

I chose once
And this was our choice.

You reply,
I also fantasize about
You.

Ingredients

there is no reason to fight. but you do it anyway.

no one will remember but you do it anyway.

unbecoming, unaccepted on all fronts

the only point every narrative agrees to is: you're a traitor

you say: i'm a traitor

you say: kill me upside down

name nothing after me

i love you this much i need this story this much.

betrayal to move all stories forward. even god accepts:

betrayal moves our worlds forward

the betrayer is militant

she needs money for shoes
she loves someone so much
she doesn't believe in god likes silver more
she believes this is the only way he can return
she is committed to paying bills
someone he loved asked him
something inside said: go ahead
she will live with the threats
they will live with what they will have to say
denounced she wanted to pay their bills and
someone they loved asked

"an open rejection of God's love"

who is this character

who are they and who did they love instead

let's be honest the world is not shaped by your tomato gardens: your good intentions

the forests grew only when we were not present

they are dying because we are murderers

the sky will turn every color and still

they will say everything is fine everything is fine

so

        desecration. of a them that we know is an us.

there is no voting white supremacy out of anything:

there is no voting white supremacy out of anything!

I made you to help me

I made you so that you could do

The extra tasks I could not

Do you understand

I made you to help me

Disclaimers for Debt

I. The Book of Revelations: Lessons Against Assimilation

I. Close Reading Revelations:

         The Consequences of Assimilation

I. Easy, Easy metaphors—

I. Everlasting judgments

         commentaries on borrowing practices

I. Dear Property:

I. *It/What always feels like mine.*

I. An informer too long! To be distinguished as anything but

Public Key:

The traitor isn't misunderstood ok?

She's deranged

She's in love the wrong way

your wounds never ending

what figures like Rachel Dolezal and types like her do not understand is
what if our political commitments had no immediate, visible, legible, reasonings?

What if instead of: I am a "black" woman and therefore I fight for Black lives

she said: *divest destroy revolt*

submit

I am committed to the fundamental destruction of
I will fight even though you cannot imagine why I might side this way
I fight regardless of whether or not my reasoning might be accepted as reasonable or not
I fight against my birthright. You do not understand but it is not for your story.

I am diverging permanently from your story.

haha am i romanticizing the traitor?

then let's leave judas out of this

and focus on what it means to destroy this self

I'm not going to turn on you. things like that don't just happen—

treachery is not a moment

but a lifetime commitment.

she's a traitor because

she owed them everything

(the woman who gives Joshua everything—

what was her name?)

Samson is the conclusion because

it's the citation that: crushed her kind.

World—

I find all your villains to be

Unreasonable

Unbelievable. Awkwardly

Constructed with too much coffined potential.

Except your white male CEO

Him. Him is true

Him you haven't constructed at all

Psalm

you don't have to study to have
regardless of work there is a home
love is not a condition for safety
survival is possible so survival is guaranteed
more

          more
is sequestered
punishment is what was once enacted but
can no longer be imagined.
an enlarged footnote—for memories
Love is not the condition for safety
but becomes a possibility

                    Amen

On the Name

the feminine ending misplaced, the honorific forgotten:

that which refuses to surrender

the names submerged deep in our bones

their names their names

to be called

their names only their names

                                        forever & ever

                                                &

                                                into the next—

I am gravely & happily indebted to the artists I've been able to work with: Mariah Starks, Michael Coleman, Justus White, Trayvond Walker, and Christopher McGill. Your originalities astonish me: my favorite memories involve our summers. My friends & comrades & teachers have encouraged me from the beginning, supported me throughout. Particularly, Brian Reed, Andrew Feld, Shawn Wong and Chandan Reddy. Nick Twemlow reached out and read one of the earliest versions of this book—a gesture I will never forget. I thank Don Mee Choi for a poetry reading that altered my life. Dorothy Wang for clearing the way, and for her friendship. Bhanu Kapil for monsters, texts, solidarity. Sarah Gzemski and Jimena Sarno for their beautiful, imaginative designs. Carmen Giménez Smith for finding me and sharing work with me, her warmth for this project: her precise, transformative editing.

Though the technical genre of this book is poetry, it could not have existed without the training I received from Fatima El-Tayeb, Grace Kyungwon Hong and Page duBois. Everything I write is in pursuit of Fatima's approval—she is my intellectual titan. Grace brought up traitors with me at the beginning and has been a database of ideas and inquiry in my life. Page duBois has modeled for me the possibilities of ethical research and writing.

All errors are mine—all insights have been borrowed.

Brooklyn Magazine, Clockhouse, West Branch, iO Poetry, The Minnesota Review, The Iowa Review, The Seattle Review, Denver Quarterly and *Tinish* published drafts of these poems. I thank the editors for providing homes for their earlier versions.

Allia Griffin, Gelare Khoshgozaran, Kiik Araki-Kawaguchi, Lucas de Lima, Maya Mackrandilal, Erica Mena, Jennifer Tamayo, and Nikki Wallschlaeger read the babiest labors of these works—you are my art breathing space. Joel Nishimura has read every word I have ever written: I could not have dreamt up a more important friend. Sam Yim, my most precious sister who forgives me, even though she's the star.

For my brother, Joseph Sung Gi Kim, who challenges me daily & expands the fullest of loves.

For my grandmother, a farmer who loved three different gamblers (a politician, a police officer, the state) who ruined her life. Who lived her life paying off the debt of others: at seven her mother's, then her lover's, from then on till the rest of her life any and every person she loved.

For the conversations I overheard her having: the drought shrivels them up, the flood washes them away, the wild boars take them all &

the free trades. The IMF. She tells me over the phone she despises those who depend on books—they're dangerous and foolish. She sends a box of potatoes to every person she thinks could help my father. They accept and are never anywhere to be found.

When the debt collectors come when everything was taken and gone when nothing but some letters remained when no one wanted to live with her and I was in Paris she would call and describe new plans: a mandu stand, kimbap delivery service. Everyone she knew was too tired. They conserved their energies for church meetings, stall prayers. I plotted to move her to France. Maybe she could work as a cashier at the monoprix.

To be her ghost instead of with her.

All of the chemicals they demanded from her soil stitched a home at the bottom of her heart and quilted her insides bare. She moved away from the city to a praying cottage to live away from traitors. On the phone she would tell me of new money making plans: schemes of pure labor pure body pure exhaustion. Nothing but her bones.

"다음에 또 사랑하자"

poems in this current predicament to insure a meeting in her afterlife

What we want is impossible, unrealistic & non-negotiable—

Eunsong Kim is an Assistant Professor in the English Department at Northeastern University. She is the co-founder and co-editor of the arts forum *contemptorary*. This is her first book of poems.